The Man of God

(2 Timothy 3:16-17)

E W Bullinger

ISBN: 978-1-78364-496-4

www.obt.org.uk

The Open Bible Trust
Fordland Mount, Upper Basildon,
Reading, RG8 8LU, UK.

The Man of God

Contents

Page

The Man of God
(2 Timothy 3:16, 17)

```
A   a     All Scripture is given by inspiration of God.
    b         and is profitable
        B         for doctrine,
            C        for reproof,
            C        for correction
        B         for instruction in righteousness
A   a     that the man of God may be perfect,
    b         thoroughly furnished into all good works.
```

This structure shows that in A and *A* we have that which is connected with "*GOD*" while in B, C and *C, B,* we have that which is connected with His *WORD*.

The following is the explanatory key to the above: -

```
A   a     The Divinely inspired word of God.
    b         its profit.
        B  Positive: Teaching what is right.        ⎤
            C    Negative: Correcting what is wrong. ⎦ Faith

            C    Negative: Correcting what is wrong. ⎤ Works
        B  Positive: Teaching what is right          ⎦
A   a     The Divinely fitted man of God.
    b         His profit.
```

In addition to this perfection of its structure, the study of which will be amply repaid, we have another lesson taught by the use of an important "figure" of language, showing us where the Holy Spirit has placed, and desires us to place, all the emphasis.

The figure is named by the ancient Greeks ASYNDETON (*A-syn-de-ton*). It means "NO ANDS." When several nouns, verbs, or sentences are placed together, sometimes they are connected according to grammatical law by placing the conjunction "and" immediately before the last. But sometimes this law is legitimately broken for the sake of attracting our attention and marking the emphasis.

It is broken in two ways: either by using "no ands," or by using "many ands." The latter case is called POLYSYNDETON (*Pol-y-syn-de-ton*).[1]

When "MANY ANDS" are used, it is to show us that we are to dwell on each thing that is mentioned or enumerated; that each is of equal importance; there being no climax at the end.

---

[1] The author has in preparation an important work on the whole of this great, but sadly neglected subject, in which he will give upwards of two hundred of these figures, each with many examples from the Word of God. (Editor's note: This can be seen in Bullinger's book *Figures of Speech ion the Bible*.)

But when 'NO ANDS" are used, it is to show us that we are *not* to dwell on the several points that are mentioned, but we are hurried on to some grand climax, which is the great point and object of the passage.

Take an example of each from this Epistle, 2 Tim. 4:17, 18,

"Notwithstanding the Lord stood with me,

- **and** strengthened me; that by me the preaching might be fully known,
- **and** that all the Gentiles might hear;
- **and** I was delivered out of the mouth of the Lion,
- **and** the Lord shall deliver me from every evil work,
- **and** will preserve me unto his heavenly kingdom."

On the other hand, look at our very chapter, 2 Tim. 3:10.

"But thou hast fully known my doctrine,
_____manner of life,
_____purpose,
_____faith,
_____longsuffering,
_____charity,
_____patience,

       persecutions which came unto me
           at Antioch,
           at Iconium,
           at Lystra;
       what persecutions I endured:

but out of them all the Lord delivered me."

These two passages both treat of the Lord's deliverance: but in the former we are detained to consider each of the wondrous facts connected with it; which in the latter we are hurried on, the Figure saying to us: It does not matter now what the troubles were, the great and blessed fact is, that the Lord delivered the Apostle out of every one of them.

This is the figure we have in the passage we now propose to study. True, the word of God is "profitable." But that is not the great point. The great point here is the object and effect, in fitting out the man of God.

It may be set forth thus: -

       "All scripture is given by inspiration of God, and is profitable
       for doctrine,
       for reproof,
       for correction,
       for instruction in righteousness,

[so] that the man of God may be perfect, thoroughly furnished unto all good works."

But, before we proceed, we must notice that the two words "perfect" and "thoroughly furnished," are cognate words in the Greek, and however the former may be rendered, the latter ought to correspond with it. If the former be rendered "perfect," then the latter should be "perfected," as in the margin. If the former is "fit," then the latter should be "fitted." The Revised Version preserves this by rendering it, "That the man of God may be complete, furnished completely unto every good work."

The adjective 'complete', Greek *artios,* means *fitted, exactly suited, specially adapted for a given use.* When used of numbers, *artios* means *even,* or *perfect.* (The adverb means *just, exactly, of coincidence of time [at the same time]*)

The verb too is important; it means as it is thus rendered *to furnish completely.* It is the technical term for *furnishing* a house or being *fully prepared* for war. In fitting out a ship for sea, everything must be thought of; every emergency must be provided for; every contingency must be considered. Calm and storm, heat and cold, fire and accident, peace and war, everything, from the least to the greatest, must be furnished. The man who has the Word of God hidden in his heart is thus "furnished completely." He is ready for every emergency. For trouble or prosperity, for friend or foe, for sorrow or joy, for attack or defence. And only such an one is thus prepared to meet the trials of life and equipped for all its emergencies.

Some passages and expressions of God's Word are important on account of the truth they convey; others derive their importance from the words employed to set forth that truth; but other passages and expressions receive their chief importance from the place in which we find them, and from the context in which they come to us.

This expression "the men of God" occurs in the New Testament only in the Epistles to Timothy (1 Tim. 6:11; 2 Tim. 3:17), and in connection with the Word of God. But why in connection with Timothy? Why not in connection with Paul? Why not in connection with Peter, or with James and John? And why in connection with the Scriptures? Why not in some other connection?

Now, the answers to these questions are full of instruction for us.

In seeking for this answer, we have to observe a principle which may be very commonly and usefully applied to all words and to all expressions (it is a very ancient rule among the Jews), and that is, that *the first occurrence* of a word or an expression is the key to its meaning and its teaching in the other parts of Scripture.

Where, then, does the expression "the man of God" first, occur in the Scriptures? We find it first in Deut. 33:1, "This is the blessing wherewith Moses the man of God blessed the children of Israel before his death."

Here we find the expression connected with Moses; not with the "blessing," but with Moses. He is the first who is definitely called "the man of God."

But then, again, why Moses? Moses was pre-eminently THE Prophet. It was he to whom Jehovah said, "I will raise them up a Prophet from among their brethren, like unto thee."

Though Christ Himself was THE Prophet, yet He was only a Prophet "like unto" Moses.

So that Moses was pre-eminently the Prophet of the Old Testament; just as Noah was pre-eminently "the Preacher." Thus our first instruction concerning "the man of God," is to place the expression in connection with the word Prophet. This brings us to our second point. What is the meaning of the word "Prophet"?

The meaning of the word is merely *to speak clearly, to bubble up;* and then *to issue forth*, hence it was used of all formal announcements.[2]

The name in the Greek is the same as the word "Prophet" in English.

The word "prophet" is just simply the Greek word transliterated, *i.e.*, spelt with English letters. Among the Greeks it was used to denote one who *spoke before*, i.e., *standing before another.* It was used exclusively of those men who stood before the Oracle or rather, before the curtain which hid the Oracle from the people.

The Oracle gave forth its unintelligible sounds, and these men who stood before the curtain professed to interpret what the Oracle said.

---

[2] There are three words used in the Old Testament.
(1) There is the *Roeh* a Seer of Visions. Samuel was known chiefly as a Roeh. See 1 Sam. 9:9: "He that is now called a Prophet (Navee) was before time called a Seer (Roeh)."
(2) The *Chozeh*, who was also a Seer, but the word refers rather to spiritual apprehension than to the actual Seer of Visions. It occurs twenty-two times, and is used of Gad, Heman, Iddo, Asaph, Jeduthun, Amos, etc.
(3) And the more common word *Navee* occurring over three hundred times.
In 1 Chron. 29:29 we have the three words in one verse, "they are written in the Book of Samuel the Seer (*Roeh*), and in the Book of Nathan the Prophet (*Navee*), and in the Book of Gad the Seer (*Chozeh*)."

But, in the New Testament, it is used of the man who *stands before God*, of the man who *speaks before* Him, and thus it is connected with "the man of God." The word "Prophet" does not mean merely to foretell future events (neither in the Greek nor in the English), but *to speak before, to speak forth, to propound, to announce.*

The meetings of the Clergy and others for prayer, and the reading of God's Word, in the days of Queen Elizabeth, were called "prophesyings," and when Jeremy Taylor called his well-known work *The Liberty of Prophesying*, he merely meant the liberty of preaching.

So that the sense of *foretelling*, in which we almost exclusively use the word in our day, is a departure from its original use. It is only by bearing this in mind that we can gain instruction from it.

But where does the word "Prophet" first occur in the Scriptures? Who is first called a Prophet?

Not many, perhaps, would be able to answer and say that Abraham was the first who is called a Prophet, and that not by man, but by God Himself. In Gen. 20:7, God says to Abimelech, "Now therefore restore the man his wife; for he is a Prophet, and he shall pray for thee."

Where are the prophecies of Abraham? There are none. He merely walked before God (Gen. 17:1) and witnessed for God.

He was recognised as *God's man* by the men of his day; he was the man who lived before God and walked before God and spake before God.

John the Baptist was, in the same sense, a Prophet.

The Lord Jesus bears testimony concerning him that he was "more than a Prophet" (Matt. 11:9); he was "called the Prophet of the Highest" (Luke 1:76); and again, "among those that are born of woman there is not a greater Prophet than John the Baptist (Luke 7:28).

And yet, where are John the Baptist's prophecies? There are none. No, he was, and was recognised as God's man, "for all hold John as a Prophet" (Matt. 21:26); he *spoke for* God, he reproved; he rebuked, he exhorted, he was God's spokesman in this world, and hence, he was a Prophet indeed.

Again, when the Lord said to the woman of Samaria, "Go, call thy husband," and thus shewed that He knew her past and present life, she said, "Sir, I perceive that thou art a Prophet" (John 4:19). He had not foretold anything; he had not spoken of the future at all but he referred only to the past and the present. his words reproved her of sin, as

John reproved Herod (Luke 3:19), and thus marked him as a Prophet.

We have another instructive illustration in Exodus 7:1, where Jehovah, speaking to Moses of Aaron, says, "Aaron thy brother shall be thy Prophet." But in chap. 4:16 we have precisely the same Hebrew word used, but another translation. Jehovah, speaking of the same facts and circumstances to Moses, says of Aaron, "He shall be thy spokesman."

Now, that is exactly the signification of the word, and the exact definition of the office of the Prophet, both in the Old Testament and in the New. The Prophet was a man who *spoke for* God, who witnessed for God; and as such he was recognised by the people as a man whom God had called, whom God had qualified, and whom God had sent forth to be his spokesman in the world – hence, "a man of God."

But for one to be a spokesman for another, certain qualifications are required. If we were to appoint a deputation who should wait upon a certain person or persons on our behalf, we should have to appoint a spokesman, and we should have to see that he understood perfectly what we wanted him to say, that he understood our case and that he would put it exactly as we wished it to be put. In other words, we should have to instruct him with our words, and to fill him with the spirit that animated ourselves.

But how is a man to be qualified to be a spokesman for God? If we turn to Numbers 11, we have God's own answer to this question. The Lord had told Moses to appoint seventy men, who should assist him in bearing the burden of the people and that He would put His Spirit upon them (vs. 16, 17), and we read (vs. 25-29): "The Lord came down in a cloud, and spake unto him, and took of the spirit that was upon him, and gave it unto the seventy elders: and it came to pass, that, when the spirit rested upon them, they prophesied, and did not cease. But there remained two of the men in the camp, the name of the one was Eldad, and the name of the other Medad: and the spirit rested upon them; and they were of them that were written but went not out unto the tabernacle: and they prophesied in the camp, and there ran a young man and told Moses . . . and said My lord Moses, forbit them. And Moses said unto him, Enviest thou for my sake? Would God that all the Lord's people were prophets, and that the Lord would put His Spirit upon them."

Hence, the Prophet was a man on whom God had "put His Spirit," and whom He had thus taught what he was to say, as His witness and spokesman. He was one to whom the Lord had *made Himself known*: - "Hear now, my words: if there be a Prophet among you, I, the Lord, will make myself known unto him" (Numbers 12:6).

Here we have a further definition of the prophet. The man of God was one to whom the Lord had made himself known.[3]

In Neh. 9:30 it is written, "Yet many years didst thou forbear them, and testified against them by the spirit in thy Prophets." (Compare 2 Chron 36:12.)

> "And he did *that which was* evil in the sight of the Lord his God and humbled not himself before Jeremiah the prophet *speaking* from the mouth of the Lord."

Hence, it was the Lord who spake by his spokesmen it was the Lord who testified against them, speaking by His Spirit in His Prophets.

He it was who said to Ezekiel (Ezek. 3:17), "Son of man, I have made thee a watchman unto the house of Israel: therefore, hear the word at My mouth, and give them warning from me."

He it was said to Jeremiah (Jer. 15:19), "Thou shalt stand before me, and if thou take forth the precious from the vile, thou shalt be as my mouth."

---

[3] He was also known as "a man of the Spirit." See Hos. 9:7, margin.

Thus, we see that the prophets of the Old Testament were God's spokesmen, whom God dignified by putting His Spirit upon them, and by teaching them through His Spirit what they were to say on His behalf.

The next point for us to notice concerning the Prophets is this, that there was no provision for them originally under the Law. Every other office was defined, and its duties were described. Further, the persons who were to perform those duties were appointed, even down to those who carried the minutest parts of the Tabernacle, down to the hewers of the wood, and the drawers of water, for the service of the Lord; but there was *no place for the Prophet*.

And if Israel had walked in the way of God's commandments, if man had proved faithful to the trust committed to him (as he never has been faithful), there would never have been any need for Prophets to be raised up.

But the priestly party of that day did exactly what the priestly party of every age has done (whether in false religions or the true). Human nature has ever used the influence and position which religion has given, for its own advantages.

The priests of Israel were no exception. They soon became absorbed in the means, they were soon involved in controversies as to the right mode of dividing the sacrifices; and as to the performance of their various priestly duties.

Hence the Prophets were raised up, and this was the constant theme of their testimony.

To this our Lord more than once refers, when he says, "I will have mercy and not sacrifice" (Hos. 6:5, 6; quoted in Matt. 9:13; 12:7. See also 1 Sam. 15:22; Ecc. 5:1, 2; Micah 6:6, 8; Isa. 1:11-20; Ps. 1:8, 9, 11, 16; Gen 6:20; 7:21; Amos 5:21, 22).

For this reason, then, the prophets were raised up, and this it was that caused them always to be specially regarded as the opponents of the priestly party.

If any will be faithful spokesmen for God, it cannot but be that they must appear to be "against" man, because Jehovah's thoughts are not man's thoughts, nor are man's ways like His ways (Is. 55:8).

It is impossible, therefore for anyone to be a faithful witness *for* God without appearing to be *against* man. See how clearly this fact is stated in the opening words of the Prophet Jeremiah.

> "Thou therefore, gird up thy loins, and arise, and speak unto them all that I command thee: be not

dismayed at their faces, lest I confound thee before them. For, behold, I have made thee this day a defenced city, and an iron pillar, and brazen walls AGAINST the whole land, AGAINST the kings of Judah, AGAINST the princes thereof, AGAINST the priests thereof, and AGAINST the people of the land. And they shall fight against thee; but they shall not prevail against thee; for I am with thee, saith the Lord, to deliver thee." (Jer. 1:17-20.)

Hence, the prophets were never popular; they were men who must never shrink from danger; they must never mind reproach; they must never be too careful of their own reputation; they could never swim with the stream; their path could never be easy and smooth; they could never look upon success as their end; or make popularity their aim.

The measure of their success was the measure of their faithfulness before God, as His spokesmen.

Their success could not be measured by the way in which their testimony was received. They must not regard the "fear of man," neither must they seek the "praise of man"; they were *men of God* and they were to fear only Him and to seek only His praise.

And now we come to another very important link in this chain of testimony: - *This is exactly our position here in this world* today.

The last words of Jesus our Lord come echoing down the ages, "Ye shall be witnesses unto Me." (Acts 1:8.)

When He had spoken these words, He was immediately taken up to Heaven and received out of their sight. Thus, His last words were, *"Ye shall be witnesses unto Me."*

God's people, now, are therefore His spokesmen, called to witness for Him during the time that Christ is absent and while God is silent.[4]

See how this is emphasised. When Paul was raised up and sent forth, his commission was, "Thou shalt be His witness unto all men of what thou hast seen and heard" (Acts 12:15). In Acts 26:16, the Lord says to him, "I have appeared unto thee for this purpose, to make thee a minister and a witness." Peter also speaks of himself as "an elder and a witness." (1 Pet. 5:6.)

There was only one Who could be called "the faithful witness." (Rev. 1:5.) We, indeed, may be "witnesses." but only the Lord Jesus could be called the "faithful witness,"

---

[4] God is now silent, but a time is coming when He will again speak from Heaven. Ps. 50:1-3; 83:1, etc.

perfect in this as in all beside. When He stood before Pilate, He said (John 18:37), "To this end was I born and for this cause came I into the world, that I should bear witness unto the truth." And, truly, we may say, "For this end are we born again, and for this cause are we sent into the world to bear witness unto the truth." This is our mission; this is our work; this is our office; and this is our duty – to bear witness unto the truth, *i.e.*, to Christ, who is the Truth, the living Word (John 14:6). And to that Word which is Truth (John 17:17) – the written Word.

"Ye shall be witnesses unto Me." That is to say, unto a Person: not merely to a creed, or to doctrines, but a living, crucified, risen, and coming Saviour. "Ye shall be witnesses unto Me."

The Gospel is merely the good tidings about this Saviour.

Our commission, now, is not to *adapt* the Gospel to every century, but to "*preach* the Gospel to every creature."

This preaching of the Gospel to every creature is to be unchangeable; it is to be one gospel for all countries, and for all ages, and for all conditions of men. Notice how the Lord immediately goes on to define the spheres of this witness – three concentric circles.

There was first of all the inner-most circle, "Jerusalem and all Judea"; that was the place where they had the

Scriptures and professed to know them! They had the Temple, and professed to draw nigh to God, though they drew nigh with their lips only, and not with their hearts. This, therefore, was the place of religiousness.

Then the next outer circle was "Samaria." Now it is written of the Samaritans (2 Kings 17:33), that "They feared the Lord, and served their own gods." This, therefore, was the place of *corrupt religion.*

And then, there was the outer circle – "the uttermost part of the earth." This was the place of *no religion.*

Now observe that it was not one gospel for one and another gospel[5] for another, but it was the same gospel for each; the same gospel for the places of religiousness, or corrupt religion, as for the places of no religion. He told them "Ye shall be witnesses unto *me.*" And then, thank God, they had the same promise that Jeremiah had. The Lord promised to be with him; he was not to fear them; they would try to kill him, they would even put him in prison, and in the dungeon, as they did; but, "I am with thee, saith the Lord, to deliver thee" (Jer. 1:19), was the gracious promise. And is not that the same promise of Christ to His witnesses now?

---

[5] Editor's note: Notice Paul's condemnation of 'another' gospel in Galatians 1:6-10.

They were commanded to go into all the world and preach the gospel to every creature and they have this promise: "Lo, I am with you always (all the days), even to the end of the world (age)."

Now, let us enquire, what is the word that most clearly and most distinctly sets forth this especial character of all Christian service, as witnesses for God? It is the word *Protestant*. The first syllable "*pro*" is the same as the first syllable of the word "Prophet," and it means *before* or *for*, just as the word "*pro*" in the word "prophet." *Testes* means a witness, and "*Testans*" means "witnessing"; so that a true Protestant is one who *witnesses for* God; he is God's prophet, God's spokesman, God's man, "the man of God." He is the one who obeys the last command of Christ, "Ye shall be witnesses unto me."

But this is the word that man will not have today. This is the word which many who profess to follow Christ are ashamed of. Oh, what a silent testimony is this to the corruption which is so rapidly increasing in all lands. Other names are used; other names are cherished; but they are not the Divine names. We call ourselves "Christians," but that is not our distinctive name. In the Scriptures only three times are the Lord's people called Christians, but not by Himself. Once we read they "were called Christians, first in Antioch" (Acts 11:26); once as a term of reproach by Agrippa, "Almost thou persuadest me to be a Christian" (Acts 26:28); and once when Peter exhorts those who suffered as "Christians," who, in the midst of the persecution under Nero, were accustomed to hear the cry of, "The Christians to the lions!": "If any man suffer as a Christian, let him not be ashamed" (1 Peter 4:16). It was the name of reproach and derision which was given to God's people by others.

Another word that so many persons are fond of using in the present day is the word "Churchman;" but that word does not occur in the Scriptures, neither does it occur in the Prayer Book, except once in the Royal Declaration prefixed to the Thirty-nine Articles, where it is used of the "Bishops and Clergy in Convocation."

Some retort that the word "Protestant" is not found in the Prayer Book. But there is something far better. There is the thing, if not the word. There is the unvarying desire to refer everything to the supreme authority of the Word of God and the faithful witness to Reformation truth. The word, however, does occur in the Coronation Service.

"Churchman" standing by itself means very little indeed: it too often means a *man of the Church*, instead of "a man of God," or "a man of Christ."

There are two words in the New Testament Greek, very similar in their signification,[6] one of them meaning *to be a prophet*; the other, *to be a witness*. These taken together are used by the Holy Spirit upwards of eighty times of God's servants. And yet, we see that the word "Protestant," which embodies the essence and meaning of both these words (which are the words of Holy Scripture, is the very word which man will not have.

Other names are multiplied and emphasized, but the name which gives us God's view of our standing and duty, that is the name which man is ashamed of. Not only is he ashamed of it, but he is ignorant concerning it. It is popularly supposed to date from the time of the Reformation as a name connected with the Reformers, but it dates back at least to the fourth century, and is probably far older, as old as the Latin language itself. It is found in the Latin Vulgate of Jerome (which was a version made in the year 385), and also in the Papal Vulgate of today. The passage is 2 Chron. 24:19: "Yet he sent prophets to them to bring them again unto the Lord; and they testified against them; but they would not give ear."

The words "testified against them" are, in the Latin, "*quos* PROTESTANTES *illi,*" *i.e.* in other words, *who*

---

[6] *Propheteuo* to be a prophet (*i.e.* a spokesman); *martureo*, to be a witness.

were Protestants! Thus, we have here the very word *"Protestant"* identified and connected with the Prophets of Jehovah, whom He sent to witness for Him, while so many were witnessing against Him.

Now we are prepared for our last point, viz., to see how it is that this term is connected with the words "the man of God." "The man of God" was the people's name for the Prophet in the Old Testament. The people recognised in him the man who had been sent by God, and they spoke of him continually as "the man of God." All through the historical books this is the popular term for the Prophets. This is the meaning of the expression as we find it in the Epistles to Timothy.

Now we are prepared to understand why this expression is used in connection with Timothy. For how are we to be qualified as God's spokesmen? If we are determined henceforth to be faithful witnesses for God, how shall we know what He would have us say? How shall we discover the testimony that He would have us give? *Only from the Scriptures of Truth!* That is why you find the expression "man of God" in connection with the declaration, "All Scripture is given by inspiration of God, and is profitable for doctrine, for reproof, for correction, for instruction in righteousness." And why? Why is it given by inspiration of God? Why is it profitable? Because God's spokesman is to be thoroughly furnished, furnished completely.

We have seen how "the man of God," who has the Scripture hidden in his heart is like a vessel equipped for every emergency: yes, only he and he only is fitted out and completely furnished so as to be able to meet all the dangers of these last days.[7] Studying the books of men, you may become a *Man of Men*, but it is only by studying the Book of God that you can become a "Man of God."

And here we have the answer to our first great question. Why is the term "the man of God" used only of Timothy? Timothy was one who knew the Scriptures from his youth, and only he who has them and has learned them and been assured of them (v. 14) is qualified to be God's spokesman and can know what God wishes him to say.

If we are to be God's spokesmen now, we must be acquainted with the teachings of God's Word, so that others seeing us and hearing us may take knowledge of us that we have been with Jesus, and recognise us as men of God.

"It is required in stewards that a man be found faithful" (1 Cor. 4:2). *Faithfulness* is the only standard that will be applied to our witness-bearing in the day that is coming. It will be said to us, not, "Well done, good and *successful*

---

[7] It is in connection with these that this reference to the Scriptures is introduced. See the former part of the chapter (3:1-9)

servant," but, "Well done, good and FAITHFUL servant."

Popularity is not to be our aim; success is not to be our object; results are not to be our guide; we are called to be faithful in our testimony, regardless of results. Faithfulness is to be the guide of our conduct, if we would hear in that day, "Well done!" This alone will be true "success."

In 1 Tim. 4:6 the Apostle charges Timothy, "If thou put the brethren in remembrance of these things, thou shalt be a good minister of Jesus Christ." So that, whatever "these things" were they were a test of Timothy's ministry.

And what were "these things"?

You have them in the verses immediately preceding: -

"Now the Spirit speaketh expressly, that in the latter times some shall depart from the faith, giving heed to seducing spirits (or deceiving spirits, *i.e.* evil angels) and doctrines of devils (teachings of demons), speaking lies in hypocrisy; having their conscience seared with a hot iron; forbidding to marry, and commanding to abstain from meats."

We have all the principles that mark the false Babylonish religion in the false Romish religion of today.

Thus, fellow Protestants, the work of a "good minister" is to "put the brethren in remembrance of these things."

Let us conclude this Bible study by summing up the various links in the chain of evidence and testimony: –

1. that the "man of God" was the prophet,
2. that the prophet was a spokesman,
3. that the office and duty of the spokesman is the special duty of all whom God has called and sent,
4. that this duty has its necessary qualifications, which consist of the *Spirit of God* and the *Word of God*.

May the Lord enable us to heed this testimony, to have these Scriptures of Truth so hidden in our hearts that we may be faithful witnesses against all that is causing the ecclesiastical corruption of the present day and bringing about us all those evils which we so earnestly deplore.

May we all be from henceforth more devout students of Scripture – God's written Word – that so we may be more faithful witnesses of Jesus, the living Word.

Also on
The Man of God

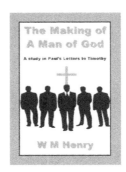

The Making of A Man of God
A Study in Paul's Letters to Timothy
By W M Henry

If the *Man of God* is not to be diverted from the truth into wrong behaviour or incorrect beliefs, he must keep away from corrupting influences. In the two letters to Timothy, there are six potential dangers that Paul identifies as pitfalls to be avoided. In each case he suggests a positive alternative, an approach that helps us see the issues more clearly.

For example, the first three dangers are all barriers to the growth of true godliness in the life of the *Man of God*. They divert us away from the thought patterns and priorities that are critical to the pursuit of godliness.

- Rather than follow a futile self-discipline, Timothy is instructed to train himself for godliness.
- Rather than seeking to develop his earthly wealth, Timothy must work for the "great gain" that comes from godliness with contentment.
- Rather than allowing the desires and passions of youth to be the dominant features of his thinking and conduct, Timothy must pursue the development of godliness; i.e. righteousness and faith in his relationship with God, and love and peace in his relationship with men and women.

After each section there are a series of questions, either for personal meditation or for group discussion, making this an ideal publication for house groups to use.

A paperback edition of this book is available from **www.obt.org.uk** and from

The Open Bible Trust,
Fordland Mount, Upper Basildon,
Reading, RG8 8LU, UK.

A newly typeset edition, well presented in an easy to read format, is available as a KDP paperback from Amazon.

It is also available as an eBook from Amazon and Kindle

ABOUT THE AUTHOR

Ethelbert W. Bullinger D.D. (1837-1913) was a direct descendant of Heinrich Bullinger, the great Swiss reformer who carried on Zwingli's work after the latter had been killed in war.

E. W. Bullinger was brought up a Methodist but sang in the choir of Canterbury Cathedral in Kent. He trained for and became an Anglican (Episcopalian) minister before becoming Secretary of the Trinitarian Bible Society. He was a man of intense spirituality and made a number of outstanding contributions to biblical scholarship and broad-based evangelical Christianity.

Some of the works of E W Bullinger published by The Open Bible Trust include:

The Transfiguration
The Knowledge of God
God's Purpose in Israel
The Lord's Day (Revelation 1:10)

For details of the above,
and for a full list of his works
published by The Open Bible Trust, please visit

www.obt.org.uk

All of the above are available as KDP paperback,
from Amazon
They are also available as eBooks
from Amazon and Apple.

ALSO BY
E W BULLINGER

THE FOUNDATIONS OF
DISPENSATIONAL TRUTH

This is Bullinger's last book and is his definitive work on the subject of dispensationalism. It covers the ministries of ...

- the prophets,
- the Son of God,
- those that heard Christ, and
- the ministry of Paul, the Apostle to the Gentiles.

He comments on the Gospels and the Pauline epistles and has a lengthy section on the Acts of the Apostles, followed by one explaining why miraculous signs of the Acts period ceased.

A hard-back edition is available from **www.obt.org.uk** and from

The Open Bible Trust,
Fordland Mount, Upper Basildon,
Reading, RG8 8LU, UK.

A newly typeset book, well presented in an easy to read format, is available as a KDP paperback from Amazon

It is also available as an eBook from Amazon and Kindle

THE TWO NATURES IN THE CHILD OF GOD
By E W Bullinger

The Bible sees the Christian as having an 'old nature', inherited through generation from Adam, and a 'new nature', bestowed through regeneration by God.

The names and characteristics of each are many and various, including "the natural man" and "the old man" over against "the divine nature" and "the new man".

The conflict between the two natures is discussed with details of our responsibilities regarding each, and the ultimate end of the old and new natures.

Finally, practical suggestions are made for dealing with the old nature.

This book is published by The Open Bible Trust.

It is available as an eBook from Apple and Amazon and as a KDP paperback from Amazon.

About this book

The Man of God

This book is an excellent, detailed and helpful exposition of 2 Timothy 3:16-17. Not only is

"All scripture *is* given by inspiration of God."

It is profitable for

"for doctrine, for reproof, for correction, for instruction in righteousness."

And its purpose is so that

"the man of God may be perfect, throughly furnished unto all good works."

And there is so much in this book of Bullinger's which will inspire and benefit, enable and encourage, the 21st Century Christian to walk more worthy of our Saviour, Jesus Christ and become a "man of God".

Made in United States
North Haven, CT
13 August 2024

55969361R00024